A Doorway to Silence

To Jean
friend, and companion in the rosary

A Doorway to Silence

The Contemplative Use of the Rosary

ROBERT LLEWELYN

Paulist Press
New York/Mahwah

This book was first published in 1986 by Darton, Longman & Todd Ltd, London.

Author's royalties earned by the sale of this book are being given to The Julian Shrine, c/o All Hallows, Rouen Road, Norwich, UK.

ISBN: 0–8091–2900–0

First published in the United States of America by Paulist Press
997 Macarthur Blvd.
Mahwah, N.J. 07430

Printed and bound in Great Britain

Contents

Acknowledgements

I would like to thank the Carthusian Order in Great Britain for permission to include an extract of patristic writings selected and translated by the Carthusians for their own use.

I am also grateful to the Revd. Roy Akerman for his help over the drawing of the prayer-stool on p. 62.

Preface

If you are unfamiliar with the rosary you need not be alarmed as you take up this book. You will find nothing assumed.

If you turn to page 10 you will find an illustration of the rosary and on the previous page a description of how it is said. On the preceding pages the accompanying prayers are set out in full.

But you do not have to use the traditional prayers if you are not at ease with them. You may feel free to change the baby's clothes if you wish, but until you have read this book do please hold on to the baby.

The baby is, of course, the rosary itself which is offered here to Christians of all denominations for the strengthening and deepening of their prayer life. If you wish to begin by buying a rosary then it may help to turn at once to the Appendix on page 82. Until you receive it you may be helped by using your ten fingers for the decades. These are explained on page 9.

Readers who are looking for meditations on the fifteen mysteries associated with the rosary will not find much mention in the present book. They are set out briefly on page 28 together with the corresponding scriptural references. Their importance to many is unquestionable. There are, however, already many good books expounding the mysteries and to one or other of these the reader must be referred.

Preface

In his book *Rediscovering the Rosary*, Gabriel Harty OP writes: 'Beginners in the rosary will concentrate on each mystery and try to picture the scene and message of the Lord. But those making progress in the way of mental prayer will use the rosary to still the mind and rest the heart as they enter the presence of the true God and Father of men. Many have given up the rosary because they feel they "cannot meditate". The fact is that through the rosary they may have gone beyond the stage of meditation and entered the restful state of contemplative prayer.' It is for such people that this book is mainly intended. Contemplation takes us into the very heart of the communion of saints. Meditation is a preliminary stage preparing us for the deeper relationship God has in store.

The principle of the rosary is more important than any particular use to which it may be put. It is the purpose of these pages to make clear how this is so and to offer different patterns of prayer to meet a wide variety of needs.

But this is not just a book about the rosary. It explores the silence beyond and the ways in which it may best be used. In addition the book affirms – among other subjects close to the prayer life – that a right understanding of the nature of God's love is essential if prayer itself is to be authentic.

ROBERT LLEWELYN
The Julian Shrine
c/o All Hallows
Rouen Road
Norwich

Introduction

In a recent book I devoted a few pages to the saying of the rosary. A number of people have told me how much this section meant to them, saying that they have since returned to it or begun to use it for the first time. I am thus encouraged to write at greater length, believing that in this practice and in the silence which must inevitably lie beyond it, a surge of new spiritual life affecting Church and nation may be generated. Some will think this a surprising thing to say. Probably, many will consider 'the telling of the beads' a senseless thing to do. I believe, however, that if you will but allow yourself to become a fool for Christ's sake it may not be long before you find yourself in hitherto unexplored country wherein your life will be enriched and your perspectives enlarged.

I referred in my earlier book to a Catholic newspaper which had described the rosary as 'merely a monotonous and boring relic of past ages when few could read'. Reciting the rosary, in common with much prayer, may certainly be monotonous and boring. It is that word 'merely' which is so absurd. It is like saying that you, the reader, are merely flesh and blood and bones.

It is just because prayer may be monotonous and boring that it provides such a splendid opportunity for patience to grow. There can be no Christian life unless it be rooted in patience. Patience exercised in love was the supreme quality of the passion of Jesus and although we sometimes say – using a convenient shorthand – that we are saved by Christ's sufferings, what we mean is that we are saved by the patience in which his sufferings were borne. Mere suffering can save no one, neither oneself nor anyone else. Patience may be defined as that quality of life which makes suffering creative;

and impatience as that whereby suffering becomes a destructive force. The choice before the Christian is not whether he shall suffer or whether he shall not, but whether, given suffering, it shall be enlarging and enriching to the Body of Christ, or dwarfing and stunting. Each of us is a member of that Body and shares its fruits. Creative suffering can shake the world. And prayer, exercised in patience, is that which fuels it.

The rosary, in something like its present form, has been in use in the Western Church for almost a thousand years, and a custom which has so universally stood the test of the centuries should not lightly be discarded. Much of our prayer life will lie the other side of the rosary but without its use (or the use of something similar) it may be that many will never discover the country beyond. The prayers and structure of the rosary are unique to the Christian Church, but the principle is common, if not universal, beyond the Christian faith. Our awareness of this should serve to enhance its value.

The rosary has been, for many, a way in to silent prayer. The silence of the heart before God is of the essence of the prayer life. It is well for newcomers to the rosary to understand this. We start with the mind gently enfolded in the words (or it may be resting in one of the mysteries) and very properly they are the focus of our attention. After a while that focus is likely to begin to disappear from consciousness, and this is where the beginner may become alarmed. What is happening, however, is that – so long as the intention to pray remains – the heart is being drawn gently into the silence beyond the words. The quality of the silence which may be ours when the words have dropped away completely at the end of the exercise will itself be proof that this process has been taking place. Anyone who is experienced in the use of the rosary will at once understand the significance of what is being said. The newcomer will probably understand only after becoming acquainted with the practice.

It is advisable to say the rosary plainly and simply as an offering to God without introspective glances to inquire whether what we are doing is meaningful or not. The exercise, if it is to be begun at all, must be begun in faith and it is in the power of faith that it is to be carried through. As the title of our book indicates, the practice is in itself (or readily lends itself to become) a contemplative activity, the silence beyond, for those called to it, being simply a deepening of what has gone before, opening ourselves yet more fully to the 'impact of the truth which is in Jesus'.[1]

The rosary is a 'little way', asking of us no more than the simplicity of children, but to those practised in it it offers a rich reward. This, however, may never be seen as an individual possession for it is of the very nature of love to radiate light and peace and joy and to spend itself quietly in helpful and practical ways. It is thus that the life of society is transformed, the leavening of the lump from within working what no government fiat could ever achieve. And so it must be that the witness of the Church will always be to the priority of prayer if its influence is to make impact on society as a whole. It would be foolish to urge that the use of the rosary was more than one of a number of ways, though it is one which is eminently simple, practical and convenient. Those well versed in it need no persuasion of its power to quicken life at its roots and to centre us once more upon God when we have fallen away. For the newcomer, let him or her go forward boldly in faith, allowing experience to teach what it is partly beyond the power of words to make plain.

Introductory reading

A peasant woman telling her beads

The French writer Maréchal has a beautiful description of an elderly peasant woman telling her beads before the cottage hearth. He writes:

'The monotony of these repetitions clothes [her] with physical peace and recollection, and her soul, already directed on high, almost mechanically, by her habitual gesture of drawing out the rosary, immediately opens out with increasing serenity on unlimited perspectives, felt rather than analysed, which converge on God.

'What does it matter then if the [humble soul] does not concern herself with living over and over again the exact meaning of the formula which she is repeating?

'Often she does better, she allows herself to rise freely into a true contemplation, well worn and obscure, uncomplicated, unsystematized, alternating with a return of attention to the words she is muttering, but building up in the long run, *on the mechanized basis they afford* a higher, purified personal prayer.'[1]

We must learn to be

If you want to learn to pray, you must understand that being is more important than doing.

It is not that doing is unimportant. It is rather that right doing springs from right being.

Much of our doing does not spring from our being. Instead of expressing our being our doing often disguises it.

When our being is firmly rooted in Christ our doing will no longer mask our being. It will be as good fruit springing from a good tree rooted in soil which is good.

God is the ground of our being. Through prayer we become rooted in him who is our ground.

When we are rightly grounded, our whole nature – bodily, mental and spiritual – will be integrated or made whole. Our experience of discord will be replaced by one of harmony.

Foundations

In learning to pray, you must first of all want God's will to be done. But you will say that only the saints can truly want that. The point is taken. The most we can do is to want to want God's will for ourselves and others. Let us leave it there and be content.

Secondly, you must understand that only the Holy Spirit can teach you how to pray. Perhaps he may help you through people or through events or books, or he may use other means. But finally he alone can be our teacher.

Thirdly, you must, so far as it is given you, be resolved to go to God for his sake and not your own. None of us can really do that. But we can keep it as something into which we may grow, and understand that regularity in prayer, especially on our bad days, largely depends on it.

And lastly, you must know that prayer and living can never ultimately be separated. Prayer can never be disengaged from the total offering of life. Prayer and daily living will be continually reacting upon one another until life ultimately becomes a single whole. In the words of an ancient teacher, life is to become 'one unbroken prayer'.[1]

Spiritual dynamite

In the handling of the rosary – it will seem foolishness to some – we are handling dynamite; not the terrorist variety which blows to pieces flesh and blood, but the more deadly type which wars against the cosmic powers of evil.

Their existence need not unduly alarm us. See the devil (if you allow him) and his angels, not as the opposite number of God, but of Michael and *his* angels, and you will cut him down to size.

In our everyday actions we are up against symptoms, whereas in the world of prayer we come to grips with the causes which lie behind.

You do not need much medical knowledge to know that rather than pacify the rash it is more sensible to deal with the agent which is bringing it about.

We are, of course, powerless to do anything of our own. But I cannot be alone in finding that, in the saying of the rosary, there steals into the consciousness an awareness by faith that one is not alone but in fellowship with Christ and his saints.

In invoking Mary we are calling to our aid the whole company of heaven.

A remarkable ministry

In these days in which we consider useful work to be that which can be displayed for all to see, we do well to remind ourselves that there have always been unseen helpers engaged in the warfare of the spirit whose victories are unlikely to become known so long as we remain on this side of death.

Last year I was visited by a religious from another country who was called to the work of intercession in a remarkable way. Often, she told me, as she prayed in her room she would be taken into scenes of tragedy or evil, where (often with tears) she, with other spirits from the other side of death, would pray for those caught up in the situation.

Her experiences, uncommon though not unique, illustrate in graphic form what is regularly being accomplished, albeit unknown to themselves, through the prayers of the faithful.

They serve as a dramatic reinforcement of our point that prayer takes us beyond the symptoms to the root of the evil which needs to be treated.

Could we but realize this, we would be as faithful and assiduous in our prayers for the healing of souls as doctors and nurses are in their own healing ministry.

Our own offering in prayer

It is best to see the saying of the rosary as an offering, just as the priest or nun sees the saying of their daily offices as their offering to God. The rosary is, in fact, a Little Office. It has the great advantage of simplicity. No books, no distractions in searching for hymns, antiphones, psalms and lessons, and the rosary itself can easily be carried wherever we go.

The offering is costly. Used regularly as a daily office it is in the first place an offering of time. It becomes an offering of patience (or should I say impatience?) and it needs resolution to go on.

The essence of prayer is waiting, waiting upon God, and such waiting with nothing but faith to support us can be extremely testing.

Just to offer our time to God, and to go on offering it with such love and devotion as may be given us, is an exercise of value both to ourselves and others, though the less we think of ourselves the better.

Mountaineers, we are told, climb mountains because the mountains are there; not because they want to return home with improved physique, though that, no doubt, is a side effect they do not despise.

The Apostles' Creed

The rosary may be begun with the recitation of the Apostles' Creed:

'I believe in God the Father Almighty, Maker of heaven and earth:
'And in Jesus Christ his only Son our Lord, Who was conceived by the Holy Ghost, Born of the Virgin Mary, Suffered under Pontius Pilate, Was crucified, dead and buried, He descended into hell. The third day he rose again from the dead, He ascended into heaven, And sitteth on the right hand of God the Father Almighty; From thence he shall come to judge the quick and the dead.
'I believe in the Holy Ghost; The Holy Catholic Church; The Communion of Saints; The Forgiveness of sins; The Resurrection of the body, And the life everlasting. Amen.'

If you do not know the Apostles' Creed it is suggested that you use another creed, or alternatively that you begin the rosary with the words:

'In the name of the Father, and of the Son, and of the Holy Spirit. Amen.'

But these last words are, in any case, often used to begin the rosary.

The rosary prayers

Say the rosary prayers at the speed natural to you, allowing your mind to be gently enfolded in the words. If you become aware that your mind is wandering, bring it back to rest gently in the words. Remember that any discursive activity of the mind is out of place at this time.

There are three prayers to be learnt: the Our Father, the Gloria, and the Hail Mary.

'Our Father, who art in heaven, hallowed be thy name. Thy kingdom come, thy will be done on earth, as it is in heaven. Give us this day our daily bread. And forgive us our trespasses, as we forgive those who trespass against us. And lead us not into temptation; but deliver us from evil. Amen.' (Some may prefer to use the version from the Alternative Service Book (ASB) of 1980.)

'Glory be to the Father, and to the Son, and to the Holy Spirit; as it was in the beginning, is now, and ever shall be, world without end. Amen.'

'Hail Mary, full of grace, the Lord is with thee; blessed art thou among women and blessed is the fruit of thy womb, Jesus. Holy Mary, Mother of God, pray for us sinners now and at the hour of our death.'

Five good reasons

The rosary in something like its present form has a history which goes back almost a thousand years. Forms of prayer incorporating the use of beads were known many centuries earlier, both in the Christian Church and beyond. It is thus a way which has been well and widely tested.

We may consider the following five reasons which make the rosary such a useful aid to prayer:

It breaks the time up into small elements and these can be dealt with one by one.

The pressure of the fingers on each successive bead is an aid in keeping the mind from wandering.

The breaking up into five decades (to be explained later) relieves the monotony of the exercise.

The audible repetition of the words helps to gather the attention into what is being done (though, later, you may prefer to use the rosary in silence).

The beads which remain to be worked are an encouragement to continue until the end.

How to say the rosary

It will be seen from the illustration on page 10 that the rosary consists of a circular string of beads, joined at the medallion to a short string of beads at the end of which is a crucifix. This latter string is called the pendant.

You begin the rosary by saying the Apostles' Creed (or an alternative), holding the crucifix in your hand. You then move to the first bead, holding it between your thumb and forefinger, and say the Our Father.

On each of the next three beads you say a Hail Mary, holding each in turn in the same way as the first bead. On the fifth bead you say a Gloria. It will be noticed that the first and fifth beads are separated from the other three.

The central group of beads on the pendant stands for faith, hope and love, reminding us that in every saying of the rosary we affirm anew – and look to the Holy Spirit to deepen within us – these three virtues which lie at the heart of the Christian life.

It will be seen that the circular string consists of five groups of ten beads (known as decades) separated at each end by a spaced bead.

You begin the circlet by saying the Our Father on the medallion. You then say a Hail Mary on each of the first ten beads, and you conclude the decade with a Gloria on the spaced bead.

The next decade begins with an Our Father on the same (spaced) bead and ends as before with a Gloria. And so on, until the circlet is completed. If you go round again, you take no notice of the pendant.

If you should need help in obtaining a rosary, turn to the Appendix at the end of the book.

Mary

From earliest times, Mary, the mother of Jesus, has been accorded a uniquely special place in the honour and devotion of Christians. 'I know surely', writes Julian of Norwich, summing up in one vibrant sentence the verdict of the Church, 'that she is higher in worth and grace than anyone that God has made; for no one that is made is above her, except the blessed humanity of Christ.'[1]

Yet apart from the narratives surrounding the birth and infancy of Jesus, Scripture tells us very little. Mary and Joseph find their twelve-year-old son in the temple at Jerusalem and we infer from Luke's narrative that Mary is growing in the awareness of the special vocation awaiting Jesus. She enters the story again at the wedding in Cana at the beginning of Jesus' ministry, and once during the ministry itself. The sword, which the aged Simeon had foretold would pierce her heart, is revealed in the watching hours on Calvary where Mary and John the beloved disciple are given to one another. And finally we read of Mary in prayer in Jerusalem with a small band of the faithful awaiting the gift of the Holy Spirit.

'Our Lord showed me . . . our Lady, Saint Mary, and he showed her on three occasions. The first was as she conceived, the second was as she had been under the cross, and the third was as she is now, in delight, honour and joy.'[2]

Christ and his mother united in love

Pious fancy, not all of it edifying, has not been slow to adorn where Scripture has been silent. Especially where God (and Jesus too) has been regarded as a harsh and forbidding figure, concerned with judgement and punishment rather than forgiveness and mercy, Mary has been seen as one by whose prayers the wrath of the Father may be turned from us. This is a theological aberration. For the truth is, as Julian so clearly saw (and we shall examine this later for it has bearing, too, beyond the rosary to the whole of the prayer life), that there is no wrath in God, and the prayers of Mary and the saints are joined to God's own compassionate love in quenching the wrath within ourselves, which hinders the vision of his beauty and holiness. Far from there being any conflict in desire, 'I saw', says Julian, that 'she and Christ were so joined in love that the greatness of his love caused the greatness of her grief.'[1]

'A certain kind of Marian piety sees God or Christ as angry at the sins of man, ready indeed to destroy the world, yet restrained by the prayers of Mary, the compassionate mother. Sometimes theologians bring their heavy artillery to bear on this kind of pious fancy, yet it is surely worthy of sympathetic consideration against the background of the God of wrath and reprobation. That there should be somewhere within the portals of judgement and vengeance a bearer of unconditional compassion is no small consolation to saint and sinner alike. Anyhow, Julian places the all-compassionate figure within the godhead, identifies it indeed with God's own countenance.'[2]

God's handmaid

'He brought our blessed Lady to my mind. In my mind I saw her as if she breathed – a simple, humble girl, not much more than a child, the age she was when she conceived. God showed me, too, in part, the wisdom and truth of her soul, so that I understood the reverence she felt before God her maker and how she marvelled that he would be born of her – a simple soul that he himself had made. It was this wisdom and this truth in her that showed her the greatness of her maker and the smallness of herself whom he had made. And it was this that made her say so humbly to Gabriel, "Behold God's handmaid." '

'Our Lord showed me our Lady, Saint Mary, to teach us this: that it was the wisdom and truth in her to know him as so great, so holy, so mighty, and so good. His greatness and his nobleness overwhelmed her. She saw herself so little and low, so simple and poor compared with God, that she was filled with humility. And so from this humble state she was lifted up to grace and all manner of virtues, and stands above all.'[2]

'I was taught that every contemplative soul to whom it is given to look and to seek will see Mary and pass on to God through contemplation.'[3]

13

A focus of attention

When learning to pray, it is a common practice to have a word or a sentence as a focus of attention to which the mind is turned, and to which it may return if it wanders.

This is a principle which has been familiar to Christians for many centuries. The Jesus Prayer of the Orthodox Church and the rosary of the Catholic Church are examples of it.

Frequently this focus is a single word, such as Jesus, Abba, Father, Love, or God. Whether it is a word or a sentence, it may be said aloud, or whispered, or framed by the lips and said silently, or 'said' in complete silence with the lips closed and the tongue still.

When the word or the sentence is said aloud, it is a focal point for speech or sound. When used silently, it is a focal point for the imagination.

You can also have a focal point for the eyes, such as an icon or a crucifix. Or for the touch, such as fingering the beads of the rosary. Or for the ears, such as a tune or a voice.

More about the focus

Our word or sentence helps to focus the mind, to make it one-pointed. It helps to clear the surface thoughts which may engage the mind and to still the mind in the presence of many thoughts which may present themselves in prayer.

At the beginning you may be most conscious of your word or sentence as being present in your head. It must be allowed to descend to the heart.

'Keep your mind in your heart and stand in the presence of God all the day long' is the advice of an ancient teacher.

In the imagery of the fourteenth-century work *The Cloud of Unknowing* the chosen word is to be fastened to the heart and to be seen at all times as our shield and our spear.

We may thus think of the Hail Mary and other prayers in the saying of the rosary. As a shield it is a defence in temptation and trial; and as a spear it is a means of praising God and interceding for others.

What good does it do?

What is the use of saying the rosary? There is much use. But the more you can leave your question behind, and perform your exercise in simplicity of heart as your love offering to God, the better it will be.

What is the use of falling in love? The one who does so will not stop to ask the question.

The saying of the rosary unites the soul to God. So, too, all true prayer and all activity performed in the spirit of prayer.

'I am the true Vine and you are the branches.' The faithful and regular practice of the rosary lays us open to the purging process of which the allegory speaks. Thus, in the deepening of union, is the fruit increased.

A soul united to God is by that very union, in ways seen and unseen, the most powerful force for good the world can know.

Is this vain repetition?

Some object to the rosary on the grounds that it involves vain repetition. The operative word is *vain*. What do we mean by it?

An action is vain if it does not achieve the end for which it was intended. If you give ten hammer blows on a nail and it does not penetrate the surface, then your action is vain.

But if with each blow there is penetration, however small, your action is useful and not vain.

Looked at closely, there is not even repetition. For the total situation has changed with each blow. A train going through Reading station is not a repetition of the same train passing through Oxford. For by then it is many miles nearer its destination.

Likewise, in the saying of your prayer, every recital is made from a different starting-point than before, and each one takes us more closely into the heart of God.

So often as you are tempted to think you are engaged in vain repetition, let the thought drop like a stone. There is nothing your Uncle Screwtape would like you to believe more.

So long as your *desire* to pray remains, you may be assured that all is well.

A continual deepening of spiritual quality

'We are not to think that long continuance of the same cry to God means no change. The outward expression may be the same, but the force of no two acts can ever be the same.

'The fact that five seconds ago I said, "Jesus, I love thee", wrought a change in me, so that when I say the same words again, I bring to them a stronger spirit of love and devotion to our Lord than would have been possible in the first instance.

'The first act brought me into closer and fuller union with him, and although I may not perceive it, so profound a change was wrought in me that each succeeding act makes upon my character an increasingly powerful impress, the force and effect of which is ever mounting.

'So, strictly speaking, there is no repetition. It is not the same but a different work that is done.

'Thus, as we go on in the work of prayer, the soul does not, cannot, abide in any one stay. There is a continual deepening of spiritual quality, and an intensification of love, and with love all the other virtues flower every moment into newer and richer things.'[1]

Is it merely mechanical?

Others object to the rosary on the grounds that it makes prayer mechanical. It is true that it introduces a mechanical element into prayer: but that does not matter. It is when prayer becomes *merely* mechanical that we act as robots and not as people.

There is a mechanical element in everything we do – for example, in walking down the road. The totterings of a child indicate that the mechanics have not yet been grasped. Yet walking is not *merely* mechanical. We walk as people, not as zombies.

So long as another element is always present – in the case of prayer the intention or desire to pray – the mechanical basis of the rosary is not a matter for concern, nor does it become so when the attention to the words fluctuates, as it will surely do.

The important thing is that the intention to pray remains, ourselves meanwhile attending gently to the words as the Holy Spirit enables us, knowing that the heart remains at prayer even though the mind may wander from the words from time to time.

It's the river which matters, but don't despise the banks

You will be helped if you hold this picture in mind for all repetitive vocal prayer.

The words are like the banks of a river and the prayer is like the river itself. The banks are necessary to give direction and to keep the river deep and flowing. But it is the river with which we are concerned.

So in prayer it is the inclination of the heart to God which alone matters. The words are there to assist and support this fundamental need. They are the framework in which the prayer is held.

The words are not the prayer. The prayer lies always beyond the words.

As the river moves into the sea, the banks drop away. So, too, as we move into the deeper sense of God's presence the words fall away and, (to continue our imagery), we shall be left in silence in the ocean of God's love.

The parable of the pheasant

Once when living within the pleasant surroundings of a religious community I watched through my window a large and – it seemed to me – rather old pheasant on the lawn.

It ran along the grass, took a short flight, and then, being tired, returned to earth once more. There followed a little more running, another flight and return, and so on.

In that illustration we may see a parable of the saying of the rosary. We move from one Hail Mary to the next with such devotion as God may give us, and then there may be, as it were, a short period on the wing, when the words, though still recited, recede into the background, and somehow we are taken beyond them, and held for a few moments in that stillness which is God.

And then – and this too is our point – just as the pheasant had the good solid earth to return to and support him as he moved forward again, so we have the words of the rosary to return to and be our support. The bird could not just fall into a void, and in the same way the words of the rosary prevent us from falling back into the distracting and discordant imagery which often holds our minds.

Thus the rosary may be a way in to contemplative prayer, little bursts of it as the bird made little bursts of flight.

The rosary keeps you on course

Here is another picture. Imagine you are looking over the bows of a ship, straight down into the water, as she plunges through heavy seas.

The power of the engines – standing for the power of the prayer – pushes the boat forward. The water divides and the waves come crashing back on the sides of the ship.

The waves stand for our distractions. They may make a fearful din and shake the vessel. She may pitch and roll frighteningly, but the engines go faithfully on and she makes her way steadily through the rough seas.

Finally she reaches harbour. The heavy seas have been passed through. We have certainly noticed them but they have not been allowed to hold our attention. So, in the rosary, our energy is conserved in taking the prayer forward.

If we continue faithfully with the prayer we shall at last reach the harbour where we would be.

The rosary as an aid to intercession

The rosary provides a valuable basis for intercession. In the Hail Mary we see ourselves as at the same level of need and dependence as the one for whom we pray. 'Pray for us sinners now and at the hour of our death.'

When you pray for another, it can sometimes happen that an element of superiority enters into your prayers. When you ask a third person to pray for you both, that element is eliminated.

When you pray for others, you can seldom presume to know their true needs. In asking another of deeper perception than yourself to pray, you do not have to occupy your time with the formulation of special requests.

You simply see your friend as lifted into the presence of God and surrounded by the company of heaven as you, too, are.

Your desire is that God's love shall flow unimpeded through the other as it is your hope, too, that it shall flow freely through you.

Dying, we live

As you finger each bead of the rosary it may sometimes help (and especially on difficult days) to say to yourself: 'This is a little bit of death.' What does one mean?

In saying the rosary you submit yourself to the prayers of Mary and, by implication, to the prayers of the whole company of heaven. On every bead this submission is renewed.

To ask for the prayers of another is in some measure to die to oneself. It is a renunciation of that choice which belongs to us when we pray directly for ourselves.

If you choose a book from the library you select what you want to read, what you think will be helpful to yourself. In some measure the self is asserted; it does not die.

But if you ask a trusted friend to choose for you, then you have in this respect surrendered yourself into his or her hands. A little bit of dying has taken place.

So, on each bead, having surrendered yourself to be prayed for according to the needs perceived by another, you may truly say: 'This is a little bit of death.' St Paul says, 'I die daily', and thus by many deaths we are prepared for that which is final. And with every death to self there is a corresponding resurrection into new life in Christ.

That I may know the power of his resurrection

As we say the rosary we ask for the prayers of Mary and the saints. What do we mean?

They are more perceptive of our needs than we can be. But certainly they pray that we may be incorporated more fully into Christ's own resurrection life. For this is at the heart of Christian prayer. We have already said that every rosary bead brings a kind of dying, and that with every death there is a resurrection.

I write this on Easter Day. We have sung that Judah's lion has burst his chains, a magnificent piece of resurrection imagery. God's word is resurrection, not simply immortality.

Resurrection speaks to us not only of our own destiny but of the destiny of all creation 'travailing and groaning'[1] until the day of its redemption; waiting to be transformed into 'the spiritual equivalent of its travail through the ages'.[2] The humanist believes in development, the Christian in transfiguration.

The 'empty tomb', with the grave-clothes packed with spices resting 'collapsed' where the body had lain (Jn 20:5), makes its own special contribution to the Christian faith – Christ the first-fruits, the forerunner of that which is to come.

Are we perhaps near to having further evidence of Christ's bodily resurrection? We await the carbon dating of the Shroud of Turin which many already believe to be genuine. May it be that a 'burst of radiation' at the moment of resurrection will be seen to offer the only feasible explanation for the astonishingly accurate and detailed recording of Christ's physical sufferings?[3]

Christ is risen from the tomb: he is risen indeed.

Allow the prayer to do its own work

As we say the rosary we should, as far as we can, allow the prayer to do its own work in us in the power of the Holy Spirit.

We are to learn to cast our prayer upon the waters, to let it go, to stand before it in relaxed awareness as we might stand before a work of art, allowing it to do its own work, to make its own impact on us.

In the beginning, however, we work on the prayer. It is later that we come to see the prayer as working on us.

It is as though a man takes out his boat and rows into the deep to cross some stretch of water. At this stage everything depends on him, though we do not forget that it is God who gives him the strength to row.

Later on, a breeze springs up. The oars are drawn into the boat and the sail is hoisted. The man now sails before the wind.

Some work remains for him to do. But it is now the breeze which is the dominant partner.

In saying the rosary, we may have to row all the way. Or on some days the wind may be there as we take it up.

Whichever way, it is God who is at work. Theologians speak of acquired prayer and of that which is infused. Either may belong in some measure to the rosary experience.

The fifteen mysteries

The traditional focus of attention is one or other of fifteen mysteries. A well-known saying runs: 'The beads are there for the prayers, and the prayers are there for the mysteries.'

Five are known as the joyful mysteries, five as the sorrowful, and five as the glorious. The full fifteen are covered in three rounds.

On the first round you are occupied with one of the joyful mysteries on each of the five decades.

The first mystery is that of the annunciation. Mary is asked to be the mother of Jesus. Your mind rests *gently* on this event as you move through the first decade.

Your mind does not move discursively nor analytically as you say the rosary. There is room for it to be occupied in this way but it is best not done at the time of prayer. At least, no effort should be made in this direction. But the mind may be free to move of its own accord within the mystery.

It is sufficient to have just a few simple words relating to the mystery ('Jesus is born'), or perhaps a familiar painting, held *gently* in the imagination, allowing any expansion to develop of its own accord from there. But don't be concerned that the imagery comes and goes, as it surely will.

A single round of the rosary is known as a chaplet. A complete saying covers three chaplets embracing all fifteen mysteries. (A single chaplet is recommended at first.) A plan will be found on the next page.

It is not advisable to refer to Bible passages between the decades. Bible reading is best done at quite a different time.

The mysteries

The joyful mysteries. (Monday and Thursday).
The annunciation The birth of Jesus is announced (Lk 1:26–38).
The visitation Mary visits her cousin Elizabeth (Lk 1:42–56).
The nativity Jesus is born (Lk 2:1–20).
The presentation Jesus is presented to God in the temple at Jerusalem (Lk 2:22–39).
The finding of Jesus in the Temple (Lk 2:40–52).

The sorrowful mysteries. (Tuesday and Friday).
The agony in the garden of Gethsemane (Lk 22:39–46).
The flogging (Mk 15:15).
The crowning with thorns (Mk 15:16–20).
The carrying of the cross (Jn 19:16–17).
The crucifixion (Jn 19:18–30).

The glorious mysteries. (Wednesday and Saturday).
The resurrection (Jn 20:1–10).
The ascension (Lk 24:50–53).
The gift of the Holy Spirit (Ac 2:1–4).
The mother of Jesus is taken up into heaven.
Jesus honours his mother.

For those who use the mysteries, appropriate days of the week are shown. A plan for Sundays might be:
Joyful mysteries: Advent Sunday to Sunday before Lent.
Sorrowful mysteries: Sundays in Lent.
Glorious mysteries: Easter to Sunday before Advent.

If you are not at ease with the last two mysteries, change them. They might be, for example: The Communion of Saints, and The Holy Trinity; or how you think best.

Saying the rosary in a group

The rosary lends itself to group saying. Several suggestions follow:

Where members of the group are accustomed to silence as, for example, in a religious community, it can be best for one member to say a complete decade, the others following in silence. The second decade is taken up by another member of the group and so on until each has had a turn, when the first member takes it up again.

Alternatively, the decades may be said in complete silence by all. One member is appointed to say the Gloria and the Our Father, thus bringing the group together again for the start of each new decade.

Another way is for the leader to say the first half of each Hail Mary, the rest of the group responding together with the second half: 'Holy Mary, Mother of God . . .'

Or the group may be divided into two with each half saying their portion of each Hail Mary.

One member of the group may be appointed to read a short passage of Scripture at the beginning of each decade related to the mystery of the decade. It might be a disturbance to divide this among several members, but others could take their turn at other meetings.

However, as was made clear in the Preface, there is no need to use the mysteries as you say the rosary. Attention to the things of God will tend to drop away as we are enabled more fully to attend to God himself.

The rosary before an icon or a crucifix

You may well find it helpful to say the rosary sitting or standing before an icon or a crucifix.

In that case you take up your position before the icon and while reciting the rosary allow your mind to be drawn into the picture. Do not worry if that does not happen, but just keep on looking – or seeing the picture looking at you – in relaxed awareness.

Your attention may stray from the icon to the words of your prayer and then back again to the icon. That is a normal fluctuation. But it should not stray further afield, and if it does so, you should then gently re-establish your relation with the icon (or the words).

The method can be linked with the mysteries by taking an icon of Mother and Child for the joyful mysteries, a crucifix for the sorrowful, and an icon of the resurrection for the glorious.

There are great works of art which portray the mysteries. A book which brings them together would be of service here.[1]

Some may prefer to have before them a bowl of flowers, or a tree, or a vase, or some other work of beauty. The use of the rosary is to liberate us and not restrict us.

The holding together of body and spirit

'Without entirely understanding the relation between body and soul that causes (the) special connection between thought and some mechanical activity, we know that it exists.'

Pascal spoke of the use of the rosary as the winning over of the machine, 'or the mechanical side of our nature, so that it helps instead of hindering the direction the spirit desires to take'.

We are not to mistake ourselves for pure spirit but to use the lower faculties as well as the higher.

'The world around us is one huge distraction from prayer; the very holding, the very slipping through our fingers of the beads, can be a powerful counter-distraction – on a bus, in the Tube, in the street . . .

'On a higher level this use of the beads is a part of the whole philosophy of the Church about man's nature. We are not pure spirit but composite beings made of spirit *and* matter.

'And so we need, if our prayer is to be true to our nature, to use material things: images either set before the eyes or fashioned in the imagination, the cross at the end of our beads, the blessing that makes them sacred, the prayers that we say on them.'[1]

The silence beyond the words

When you say the rosary aloud, it may be that after a time your mind no longer rests in the words, nor yet in one of the mysteries (if that is your way), nor in anything else you could name.

It is likely that your mind is resting largely in the silence which is beyond the words, which is God.

You may judge that this is so because when finally the words drop away and you are left in silence you know that this is a different quality of silence from that experienced before the exercise was begun.

If that is so, then it is evident that you were largely resting in this silence earlier when the words were still being repeated.

If you consider this, you will not be worried lest you were doing nothing, even though the words you were reciting no longer had meaning for you.

The whole object of the way of the rosary is to enable you to attend to God, and when the words have helped you to do just that, they have served their purpose and done all they were ever intended to do.

A measure of detachment in relation to the words will be found to develop of its own accord as the rosary prayer becomes more interior. The following two rules may seem strange until tested but a time may come when they will be helpful: 'Do not try to attend to the words', and 'Do not try *not* to attend to the words'.

The silent use of the rosary

The Hail Mary is, perhaps, the longest of the commonly used repetitive prayers and lends itself to silent use less easily than does a short sentence or a single word.

The silent repetition of a prayer should not be forced but should be adopted only when the user is ready for it.

When the Hail Mary comes to you in the silence, almost of its own accord, then you may profitably use it silently. At first this may generally happen immediately after a number of vocal repetitions.

Do not continue praying aloud once the silent use has been offered you. But on another occasion you may well need to return to vocal use.

There is at the beginning (and for some, perhaps, always) less strain in vocal than in silent prayer. Yet silent prayer, when we are ready for it, takes us deeper. We should be simple enough and humble enough to use vocal prayer so long as we need it.

When, in vocal prayer, the mind has in good measure come to rest in the heart (or in some other body centre, it may be), it is likely that we shall be ready for silent use. Otherwise there may be undue tiredness and strain.

The prayer and the silence beyond

Picture to yourself a group of children at play. They are so absorbed in their game that they are not conscious of the fact that they are playing. There is no unoccupied corner in the mind of any child enabling him or her to reflect, 'I am playing.'

Something similar may happen at prayer. At some stage we may be drawn into the silence beyond the words being repeated by the voice or silently in the mind. The words (or it may be the single word) drop away and we are now in the silence.

But, as with the children at play, we are not conscious of our state. The silence has so taken over that there is no room for conscious reflection on it. There is no unoccupied area of the mind which enables us to reflect, 'Now I am in silence.'

But then, just as a child may suddenly realize he is at play, so we may become conscious that we are in silence. It is at this point that the word or words of our prayer which had disappeared should be taken up again.

We are not to attempt to force upon ourselves the state of forgetful silence we have just lost. But it may be that as we go on faithfully with the prayer it will be given to us again.

In a single session this sequence may recur several times. But on other days we may not be drawn into the silence at all. By silence, here, is meant the silence beyond the silent repetition of the prayer.

The rosary and the sense of touch

A valuable focus of attention as you say the rosary is one part or another of your own body. Probably everyone may be helped by this.

You say the words of the Hail Mary which help to relax the mind but your attention is focused gently on a part of your body.

Obviously it makes special sense to direct the attention to the fingers holding the beads. As you hold each bead and say the Hail Mary your awareness goes into the sense of touch experienced by your fingers.

Nothing exists for you for the moment but this feeling of the fingers on the bead. All heaven and earth is gathered into it. As your attention strays you bring it gently back.

It may be that after a while the words get in your way. Then you can drop them and go through the whole round, simply letting your awareness be drawn into the touch on the beads.

Perhaps you will take five or ten seconds on each bead and rather longer on the beads separating the decades. Or perhaps on the separating beads you may like to revert to vocal prayer.

Be free!

The rosary is healing

But your awareness need not go into your fingers. You can go round the whole body, making each part an object of attention or awareness, saying the rosary prayers at the same time.

Thus, be aware of the heart centre. As you say the prayer, look gently towards it in the mind. Let your mind descend into the heart. You are directing the healing energy of love to that part of your body.

Then go round your body, mentally taking one or two beads for each part. Take whatever part occurs to you: the shoulders, the arms, the hands; the brow, the face, the jaw. Through your awareness of these parts direct the healing energy of love to each in turn. So far as time allows do not leave anything out.

In this way you bring healing to every part of your body; and thus to every part of yourself, that body-soul-spirit complex which makes up each one of us.

Perhaps one half of the hospital beds in the country would be emptied if everyone were to spend fifteen minutes on this each day (or on any other exercise in this book). Personally I believe it would be more than half.

And what a boon to the health service, and to every other service too. No government, of whatever party, can create a welfare state if we, the people, are failing to draw upon the spiritual resources available to us.

A walkabout may help

Often you may find it helpful to walk about as you say the rosary. Indeed, there may be days when you will know you have to do so if you are to manage to say it at all.

Especially if you are 'troubled about many things' it can be a great help to walk up and down and say the rosary aloud.

There is a physiological reason for this. The very act of walking helps to calm the mind if this is our desire and we co-operate mentally with it.

Buddhists know well the value of a meditative walk. Clergy know there can be days when it is helpful to walk about when saying their offices.

The rosary makes a good companion for a country walk. Some will say that they prefer to look at the cows and birds and trees. Others will reply that they are best able really to 'see' after a meditative period.

Attention to the actual words of the rosary is not necessary

In saying the rosary, it is a mistake to think you have to attend necessarily to the words.

It is true that attention to one point or another is required. The mind is not to be scattered or allowed to wander where it will.

It may be your way to use the mysteries when you say the rosary. In that case your mind will rest gently on some aspect of the mystery being considered. Perhaps it will be on a single word or on some painting which has appealed to you. Meanwhile you just go on saying the words, seeing them as a framework which upholds your prayer.

Or you may be using the rosary as a basis for intercession. Then your mind may rest simply on the name of the one for whom you are praying. And the words go on in the background as before.

After a while it may be that your mind returns to attend to the words. And then a little later another name or cause holds your attention.

Newcomers to the rosary are liable to feel guilty when the words slip into the background. Let them be assured that it is often necessary that they should do so.

Drugs and props

Someone tells me today the rosary is a drug. It is an escape from the realities of life. If so, then sleep, too, is a drug. Every night it opens an escape route.

Sleep restores my physical and mental energies. Such a 'drug' is welcome indeed. And the rosary quickens my spiritual life. Is it to be despised for that?

It would be better to see the rosary as a prop. We all need props if we are to survive at all. Air and food and water are three props which make life possible.

If a man breaks his leg he needs crutches. Crutches are his props until he can discard them. Yet he still needs a prop: this time, his own two legs.

A part of the art of living is to discover what props are good for us and to know when (if ever) we may dispense with them and use others. The rosary should be laid aside when it no longer helps.

The life of prayer is supported by many props evident to the senses. In church there may be a crucifix for the eyes, music for the ears, incense for the nose, bread and wine for the taste. The rosary offers a prop for the touch.

It may happen in prayer that all props have to be knocked away and we are left in the bareness of faith. Even then, faith is our prop.

A wider use for the rosary

If you are not at ease with the Hail Mary you may like to use one or more of the prayers on the following pages. Through repeated repetition, with the mind resting gently in the words, the prayer may become your 'mystery' for the time being.

This is a well-tried and ancient way of meditation whereby the essence of the text seeps silently into the unconscious, there to take root and impregnate the whole life.

Starting with the Lord's Prayer on the medallion, the text chosen is repeated on each of the decade beads with a Gloria on the spaced bead. The mind is very gently enfolded in the words and the text is allowed to melt into the heart rather as a sweet dissolves in the mouth. The actual instrument of the rosary is our aid in maintaining the exercise to the end.

You may of course like to choose your own texts. The Bible and especially the Psalms provide an almost inexhaustible supply. Or spontaneous prayers may arise from time to time.

It should, however, be noted that it takes a matter of years rather than days for repetitive prayer to become fully lodged in the heart. Too much variation is not, therefore, advisable. Those accustomed to the Hail Mary for many years may find they want no other. Yet in my experience there will be times when another prayer will suggest itself as being best able to meet one's need.

Prayers suitable for the rosary

Be still, and know that I am God (Ps 46:10).

Abide in me, and I in you (Jn 15:4).

The love of God is shed abroad in our hearts (Rm 5:5).

O God, make speed to save us (The Book of Common Prayer).

O God, thou art my God, early will I seek thee (Ps 63:1).

Like as the hart desireth the water-brooks, so longeth my soul after thee, O God (Ps 42:1).

God is our hope and strength, a very present help in trouble (Ps 46:1).

Grace, mercy and peace from God the Father and our Lord Jesus Christ (1 Tm 1:2).

Those who wait for the Lord shall renew their strength (Is 40:31).

My trust is in your mercy and my heart is joyful in your salvation (Ps 13:5).

Lord, I accept as the blessing of your great mercy all pains which make my self-love suffer and all humiliations which crucify my pride (based on Jean-Pierre de Caussade).

Rest eternal grant unto him, O Lord, and let light perpetual shine upon him.

More prayers which may be used on the rosary

My presence shall go with you, and I will give you rest (Ex 33:14).

Restore unto me the joy of your salvation (Ps 51:12).

Thou wilt keep him in perfect peace whose mind is stayed on thee (Is 26:3).

When thou passest through the waters I will be with thee; and through the rivers, they shall not overthrow thee (Is 43:2).

I will bless the Lord at all times: his praise shall continually be in my mouth (Ps 34:1).

I am the Lord that healeth thee (Ex 15:26).

Lord, if you will, you can make me clean (Mk 1:40).

Fear not, for I have redeemed you, I have called you by your name (Is 43:1).

My yoke is easy, and my burden is light (Mt 11:30).

He heals the broken in heart and binds up their wounds (Ps 147:3).

The joy of the Lord is your strength (Nem 8:10).

My grace is sufficient for you; for my strength is made perfect in weakness (2 Co 12:9).

You will show me the path of life; in your presence is fullness of joy (Ps 16:12).

Hold thou me up and I shall be safe (Ps 119:117).

Further suitable texts

Into your hands I commend my spirit (Lk 23:46).

Casting all your care upon him, for he careth for you (1 P 5:7).

Underneath are the everlasting arms (Dt 33:27).

Praise the Lord, O my soul (Ps 103:1).

O Lord, my strength and my redeemer (Ps 19:15).

O God, make clean our hearts within us (The Book of Common Prayer).

O all ye [whatever takes your fancy], bless ye the Lord, praise him and magnify him for ever (Benedicite).

The word was made flesh and dwelt among us (Jn 1:14).

Christ is risen from the tomb, he is risen indeed.

All shall be well, and all shall be well, and all manner of thing shall be well (Julian of Norwich).

Abba, or Father, or Abba Father.

Maranatha [pronounced *mah-rah-nah-thah*], an Aramaic word meaning 'Come, Lord, come' (1 Co 16:22).

O Saviour of the world, who by thy cross and precious blood hast redeemed us, save us and help us we humbly beseech thee, O Lord (The Book of Common Prayer).

God is all-loving and will do everything (Julian of Norwich).

Lord Jesus Christ, Son of God, have mercy on me, a sinner (The Jesus Prayer of the Orthodox Church).

A rosary psalm of praise

The first five verses of Psalm 103, recited twice on each decade, make an excellent round for the rosary:

'Praise the Lord, O my soul, and all that is within me, praise his holy name.

'Praise the Lord, O my soul, and forget not all his benefits;

'Who forgiveth all thy sin, and healeth all thine infirmities;

'Who saveth thy life from destruction, and crowneth thee with mercy and loving kindness;

'Who satisfieth thy mouth with good things, making thee young and lusty as an eagle.'

The five verses are then said again and a Gloria is said on the spaced bead between the decades; and so on, until all five decades have been completed.

Praise and thanksgiving

Verses from the Benedicite can well be worked on the rosary beads. The Benedicite is to be found in the Book of Common Prayer as a canticle appointed for Morning Prayer. Each verse contains the refrain: 'Bless ye the Lord, praise him and magnify him for ever.' Thus:

'O ye mountains and hills, bless ye the Lord; praise him and magnify him for ever.
'O ye children of men, bless ye the Lord, praise him and magnify him for ever.'

You can make up your own as you go along: 'O John and Mary, bless ye the Lord; praise him and magnify him for ever.'

Whatever holds your attention to attract you can thus be lifted up in praise to God, enfolded in an improvised verse of the Benedicite.

'Every creature of God is good and nothing is to be refused if it is received with thanksgiving.'[1]

'He who bends to himself a joy,
Doth the winged life destroy.
But he who kisses a joy as it flies
Lives in eternity's sunrise.'[2]

Beyond the rosary to silence

We have seen that the rosary may be a way in to silent prayer. In the following pages we move on to inquire the nature of the silence and to see how we may best use it. Two images may be of help:

You may have the image of a sentry on duty: he is alert and watchful, not simply on behalf of himself but for those whom he is given to protect.

His awareness is assisted by his posture and this, too, is an important element in prayer. Moreover, the 'shield and spear' of prayer is active not just on behalf of the one who prays but for the whole Body of Christ.

Or you may have the image of two lovers. They have already come to know about one another as we have come to know about God and Jesus through meditating on the Scriptures. They now need to know one another, a much more intimate affair. Conversation which before seemed necessary may now be superfluous. They can simply relax and *be* in each other's company. A whispered word, a glance, a touch says everything. It is not difficult to see the counterpart in prayer.

St Augustine and unceasing prayer

'Let your desire be before him, and the Father who sees in secret will hear your prayer.

'Your very desire is itself your prayer; if your desire is continued, so is your prayer also.

'It is not in vain that the Apostle says: Pray without ceasing. Does he mean when he says these words, Pray without ceasing, that we should be unceasingly bending our knees, prostrating our bodies, raising our hands? If we claim that this is our way of praying, I can well imagine that we shall not be able to maintain it without interruption.

'But there is another sort of prayer, namely desire, and this prayer is uninterrupted.

'Whatever you are doing, if you are desiring the Sabbath, you are praying incessantly even without words.

'If you do not wish to cease from prayer, do not cease from desire. Your continual desire is like a continual voice within you.'[1]

It is the intention which matters

If we were to pay attention to St Augustine's words many of our problems relating to prayer would be solved.

Basically, what Augustine is saying is: Watch your will and not your feelings.

If you are in silence and *intending* to pray, you are praying. You are not to worry if it does not feel like it.

If you are saying the rosary and *intending* to pray, you are praying whether you feel that way or not.

If you finger through the beads of the rosary in silence, *intending* to pray, then most surely you are praying.

So, too, if you are washing up, serving your neighbour, listening to music, taking a walk, eating a meal, and intending to pray (that is to say, your action has been offered to God), you are praying.

But in these last activities and the like, it is easy to lose your intention, and so you need practice regularly in the formal times of prayer. It has been wisely said that we can never learn to pray everywhere all the time until we have first learnt to pray somewhere some of the time.

For God's sake and not our own

It is good to reflect from time to time that we are to go to prayer for God's sake and not our own.

Even so, that can never be entirely true, not at least this side of death. In some degree we shall always pray to God mindful of what we get from him. Nor would God want it otherwise.

For at every point God accepts us as we are, and he will accept and purify our mixed motives when we make our daily offerings as purely as it is given us to do.

Our intention and desire to go to God for his sake will be revealed in the constancy of our prayer in those periods when feeling and mood are acting against us.

If, when the time of prayer comes round, we do not respond, except when we feel like doing so, then it is a clear sign that we go to God chiefly for what we get from him.

If, however, come what may, we faithfully respond, then God is placed first and is honoured as any lover would honour his beloved.

There is no surer test of motive or of the genuineness of our prayer life than the manner of our response when the going is hard.

Julian of Norwich on prayer

'Our Lord is greatly cheered by our prayer. He looks for it, and he wants it. By his grace he aims to make us as like himself in heart as we are already in our human nature.

'So he says, "Pray inwardly even if you do not enjoy it. It does good though you feel nothing, see nothing.

' "Yes, even though you think you are doing nothing.

' "For when you are dry, empty, sick, or weak, at such time is your prayer most pleasing to me though you find little enough to enjoy in it." This is true of all believing prayer.

'Because of the reward and everlasting gratitude he wants us to have, he is eager to see us pray always.

'God accepts his servant's efforts and intentions whatever our feelings.

'It pleases him that we should work away at our praying and at our Christian living by the help of his grace, and that we consciously direct all our powers to him, until such time as, in all fullness of joy, we have him whom we seek, Jesus.'[1]

God will give us what is best

'So easily do we pray for the wrong things:
For strength that we may achieve,
and God gives us weakness that we may be humble;
For health that we may do great things,
and God gives us infirmity that we may do better things;
For riches that we may be happy,
and God gives us poverty that we may be wise;
For power that we may have the praise of men,
and God gives us weakness that we may feel the need of him;
For all things that we may enjoy life,
and God gives us life that we may enjoy all things.
And so having received nothing that we have asked for,
but all things that we have genuinely hoped for,
our prayer has been answered, and we have been blessed.'[1]

'I saw truly that it gives more praise to God and more delight
if we pray steadfast in love, trusting his goodness, clinging
to him by grace, than if we ask for everything our thoughts
can name.

'The best prayer is to rest in the goodness of God, knowing
that that goodness can reach right down to our lowest depths
of need.'[2]

'He who seeks from God
Anything less than God
Esteems the gifts of God
More than the Giver.
Has God, then, no reward?
None save Himself.'[3]

Asking, and seeking, and knocking

Jesus says: 'Ask and it shall be given you; seek and you shall find; knock and it shall be opened to you.'[1]

In asking, I am dependent on the generosity and goodwill of another. I ask the librarian for a book and then sit down – in faith – waiting for the book to be brought to me.

But in seeking, I am dependent on the thoroughness and enterprise of my search. The book will never be mine unless I have expended my energy in finding it.

The words of Jesus, then, open up two different aspects in prayer. There is a place for asking with the simplicity of a small child and then awaiting the answer in faith.

And there is a place for seeking with the energy and thoroughness of a grown person until the object of the search is found.

In the final saying of Jesus the first two aspects are combined. The knocking represents the seeking with perseverance, while the time of the opening of the door rests upon the judgement and goodwill of the householder who is God.

Posture in prayer

You have a wide choice of posture in prayer. Sitting on an upright chair is probably the best position for most Western people, especially for the middle-aged and beyond.

The Holy Spirit first came on the Church when it was seated.

'Sitting, I am most at rest and my heart most upward. I have loved to sit, for thus I loved God more, and I remained longer within the comfort of love than if I were walking or standing or kneeling.'[1]

The back is held straight in an easy tension, the head erect, the shoulders down, the mouth lightly closed, the muscles of eyes and face and jaws relaxed, the arms relaxed, the hands resting on the top of the thighs or folded in the lap.

St Ignatius of Loyola writes: '. . . to enter upon the contemplation, at one time kneeling, at another prostrate on the ground, or lying face upwards, or seated, or standing, always intent on seeking that which I desire. Here we will make two observations: first, if kneeling I find that which I desire, I will not change to another position, and if prostrate, in like manner etc; secondly, in the point in which I find that which I desire, there will I rest without being anxious to proceed farther, until I have satisfied myself.'[2]

You have only to desire

Let me tell you a way of silent prayer which may be of great help.

It springs from our reading of St Augustine where he writes: 'Your very desire is itself your prayer; if your desire is continued so is your prayer also.'

St Augustine's words are commended to us in the final sentence (apart from the blessing) of *The Cloud of Unknowing*. The author writes: 'St Augustine says: "All the life of a good Christian is nothing only but holy desire." '

You take up your position for prayer. You allow yourself to relax and look to the heart. You keep quite still and you remain so.

You think, perhaps, that this is no prayer. You are now advised to say: 'Do I desire to pray?' The answer is yes; if not, why else would you stay? If, then, you desire to pray, you are, says Augustine, praying.

You repeat the question to yourself as often as you need to. You get it firmly in your mind that you do not even have to pray, you have only to desire to pray! And then you *are* praying!

Try this piece of foolishness. It makes tremendous sense. Others have told me the same.

Letting go, and letting be, and letting God

You must not be too confident that because a way of prayer has helped you on one day it will be the same on the next. It may be quite different.

Often it is helpful to use just two very short sentences in the silence: 'Let go' and 'Let God'.

Or you may add a third: 'Let go' and 'Let be' and 'Let God'.

The letting go applies to the tensions of the body and the letting be to the distractive thoughts which may intrude into the silence.

The rule is to allow the distractions to be there to buzz around as they will, but not to develop them or to become involved with them. You may recognize them; there is no point in pretending they are not there.

Jean-Pierre de Caussade has a helpful illustration: See yourself in the sea with stones in your hands. These are your distractions. Open your hands and let them go. Let them sink into the depths.

But, alas, they do not always do so. They behave as rubber balls and float around you. Very well, then, let them float. Do not be disturbed by them. Let the tide take them away as it will and when it will.

Meanwhile, renew your desire that God shall work in you as he pleases.

Distractions to be handed over to God

When a thought arises spontaneously during prayer it is best to see it as being handed over to God and being given to him to take care of.

Meanwhile, we are to continue with our way, recognizing the thought but not developing it or getting involved with it.

I recall how, in a Zen–Buddhist retreat, a woman troubled by memories in silent meditation appealed to the *roshi* for advice. He told her not to develop her thoughts but to let them rise to the 'Lord of the Temple'. And he added: 'They are there for your healing.'

This was an encouraging thing to say. The traditional Christian answer that distractions, if not attended to, 'can do you no harm' is too negative. This thought or memory from the unconscious needs to present itself if we are to be healed.

A saying attributed to Jesus from the Egyptian desert runs: 'If you bring forth what is within you, what you bring forth will save you; if you do not bring forth what is within you, what you do not bring forth will destroy you.'[1]

The river and the boats

Here is an illustration. It is an ancient one, taken from Zen-Buddhism.

Imagine you are on a bridge spanning a river. You are in the centre of the bridge and looking over the parapet straight down into the water.

The water flowing under the bridge represents the stream of consciousness flowing across the mind during prayer.

On the river are empty boats. These represent your distractions. They float down with the current and pass under the bridge.

Your rule is that you may watch the boats but you must resist the temptation to jump on board.

Distractions are for healing

C. G. Jung has an illuminating comment on the subject of distractions. The Jesuit priest William Johnston writes as follows in his book *The Still Point* (now out of print):

'As a therapist Jung was chiefly attracted by the healing powers of Zen. He often speaks of psychic wholeness accruing from its practice. As conflict was caused by disharmony between the conscious and unconscious mind, so this was solved by the rising up of unconscious elements. For this eruption was not an indiscriminate something popping up from the mysterious depths, but is rather (Jung's words) "the unexpected, comprehensive, completely illuminating answer to the problems of one's psychic life". Hence the resulting equilibrium and peace. Zen helps the development of healthy psychic growth, since in its silent darkness the unconscious is allowed to rise up, thus creating a deep and wealthy conscious life.'

Do not, then, feel guilty about unsought distractions. It is likely that something creative is coming to birth within you. When a mother's time is near, the doctor will not say: 'It will not harm you to have your baby.' Rather would the truth be: 'It will harm you not to have your baby.'!

Learning to receive the prayers of others

The healing prayers of Mary and the saints reach down to us on earth. It is a good plan sometimes simply to lie down flat on your back for the purpose of absorbing their prayers just as you may absorb the sunshine at the seaside.

You have, perhaps, many friends on earth who pray for you. It is part of the courtesy of prayer to make occasions for receiving what they would give you.

In either case we can receive best when we are relaxed, when the barriers erected by the mind are down.

Most foolishly we are often afraid of just lying flat. We think of it as a waste of time, or that we are being lazy.

But it needs a good deal of resolution to get down on to the floor and to stay there, quite still, even for ten minutes.

Try it as a duty since you are unlikely to do so as a choice. You will find yourself wonderfully refreshed.

Our unseen helpers

How seldom do we know our true helpers!

Seeing a motorist unable to get a grip on a frozen slope, I tried to push him free. Soon I was joined by two others.

We pushed and pushed to help the skidding wheels and soon he was speeding on his way.

Perhaps he congratulated himself on his perseverance. His rear window was thickly coated with snow and he did not know that we were behind him.

We are linked with one another and with the whole company of heaven more than we can ever know in this life.

One day, perhaps, we shall know those who have helped us.

Allowing God to carry you

You may find there are days when the best thing you can do at prayer is to take up your sitting position and try to go to sleep.

If you do this, your breathing will tend towards the same pattern as when you are asleep. It is this which is important. You will be mildly aware of this at the back of your nose and at the top of your chest. Your breathing, too, will deepen and it will seem more inward.

It is most unlikely that you will go to sleep, but if you do, it will not matter.

Perhaps we are paying God a compliment when we are so unconcerned about ourselves that we are content to nod off in his arms. Rather as we might pay a compliment to our driver on the motorway when we go to sleep at his side.

Often in prayer we get in God's way. We want to do the work ourselves instead of leaving it to him. He speaks as a doctor might speak to his patient: 'If only you would let go and leave it all to me I could do something for you.'

We shall know whether we have done right by the refreshment we shall experience when the prayer time is over.

Relax, and 'let the spirit of LIFE flow through you'.[1]

Using a prayer-stool

Many people today favour a prayer-stool. To use it you kneel down, place the stool over your calves, and sit on it. In the stool illustrated, the seat slopes slightly downwards towards the front. Many stools, however, have a horizontal seat.

The support shown in the diagram is there to strengthen the stool. But clearly other means may be devised.

If you do not have a prayer-stool you can, perhaps, sit back on your heels. If you are not at ease you can put a pillow or a cushion, or, if in church, a hassock (several inches deep) on your calves and sit on that. The advantage of a prayer-stool is that the circulation of your blood is not restricted. This may happen in other cases in an extended prayer time.

Ordinarily this position will help you to be alert and attentive. But if on some occasion you go to prayer tired, and drowsiness overtakes you, why not stretch forward and lie prone, resting your brow in your hands? It is in any case a good position for prayer. It well expresses our creatureliness before God.

But it may be that you will fall asleep. What of it? 'Those who have the gale of the Spirit', says Brother Lawrence, 'go forward even in sleep.' And you will feel greatly refreshed for the remainder of your prayer time.

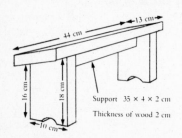

Support 35 × 4 × 2 cm

Thickness of wood 2 cm

Bereavement

A son who goes to settle in Australia can be held back in his new life if the mother he has left behind is fretting for him. He needs her blessing and asks to be set free.

Even our prayers for our friends can sometimes hinder rather than help because, unknowingly, they may serve to tie them to us, restricting their freedom rather than releasing them.

In the silence of prayer we can do no greater service than to lift our friends into the presence of God, allowing his love to enfold them.

Most of all are we likely to hinder another moving on into new life when we grieve wrongly in bereavement. It would be a denial of our humanity not to miss our loved ones, and God would not have it otherwise. But we have, too, to try to commit them into the hands of God.

Prayers for the departed can be a great help in enabling us to come to terms with grief. But, even more importantly, they can set free the other who may still be tied to earthly concerns the other side of death.

Go forth upon your journey from this world, O Christian soul,
In the name of the Father who created you,
In the name of the Son who redeemed you,
In the name of the Holy Spirit who strengthens you,
In communion with the blessed saints, and aided by angels and archangels and all the armies of the heavenly host.
May your portion this day be in peace, and your dwelling in the heavenly Jerusalem.

Mater dolorosa

'I'd a dream tonight
As I fell asleep;
Oh, the touching sight
Makes me still to weep:
Of my little lad,
Gone to leave me sad,
Ay, the child I had,
But was not to keep.

'As in heaven high
I my child did seek,
There in train came by
Children fair and meek,
Each in lily white,
With a lamp alight;
Each was clear to sight,
But they did not speak.

'Then, a little sad,
Came my child in turn,
But the lamp he had,
Oh, it did not burn!
He to clear my doubt,
Said, half turned about,
"Your tears put it out;
Mother, never mourn." '[1]

Thanksgiving

St Paul says we are to give thanks whatever happens. Probably only a saint should make such a command. Certainly only a saint could fulfil it.

If we are to take St Paul's words seriously we must first recognize that there are two kinds of thanksgiving. There is the thanksgiving of the feelings and there is the thanksgiving of the will.

It is not difficult in fair weather to give thanks to God even though we often fail to do so. We are thankful and we feel thankful.

But when things happen which are contrary to our liking we can only give thanks with the will. This cannot be done in the power of feeling. It can only be done in the power of faith.

If Paul could give thanks in his sufferings it was because in the power of faith he knew that in some way God could use them to advance his Kingdom, both within the world and in Paul himself.

Often it happens that hours, weeks, or years later we can *feel* thankful for events which, at the time, we could respond to only in the power of faith. Perhaps we can never feel thankful for some things this side of death. But as Christians we shall believe that a larger perspective awaits us.

Depression

The settled habit of praise and thanksgiving will do much to ward off depression. Nevertheless, depression is an affliction which most of us are likely to experience from time to time.

Rightly passed through, depression can be for the deepening of the spiritual life and the gateway to a fuller joy than was open to us before.

The rosary can often be of great help. But it should be noted that as we recite the Hail Mary (or the prayer of our choice) we must not try *not* to feel the depression. We must allow it to 'free-wheel', recognizing it but not voluntarily examining it, and continuing the prayer as it is given us to do.

Yet since it is a mark of depression to cloud and confuse the mind, our prayer at such times may appear to be almost or quite meaningless. We are not to be further troubled by this. The intention to pray remains and the need is to continue the prayer as best we may, allowing it to do its own work and not attempting to force the issue. The 'weight' of the depression has to be borne and allowed to dissolve in its own time.

It may help to see oneself as the captain of a ship in a fog. It is not in our power to move into the sunlight but, God helping us, it is in our power to move towards it.

But perhaps there are some fogs where all we can do is to heave-to and wait for the clear. We are not to feel guilty if there are some depressions which leave us seemingly helpless; nor then in seeking medical help, which it may well be our duty to do.

Anger, sexual desire and other emotions

Our reading on depression has application, too, to various emotions such as guilt, shame, anxiety, sexual desire and anger which may press hardly upon us from time to time.

Take the case of anger. Some frustration or contradiction has wounded our pride and sparked this temper within us. What are we to do with it?

We may repress our anger and drive it inwards. That way, however, lies bitterness and resentment, and indeed depression itself; and at some unforeseen moment the possibility of an uncontrolled and explosive outburst which may do much harm.

The alternative is to release our anger. But here, too, there is a choice. Is the release to be creative or destructive?

An irrational outburst of wrath means that the anger will be 'out' and our inner tension relieved for the time being. But the cost and shame will be unnecessary and undeserved suffering to another.

But in the rosary our anger finds *creative* release. There is a Hasidic saying which runs: 'Break your anger by compassion for the one with whom you are angry.' In the saying of the rosary this transformation is taking place.

So, too, we may be helped in the area of sexuality. Without neutralizing sex at the physical level, the rosary works to transmute this part of our nature into compassionate love and spiritual joy.

Making the necessary substitutions, paragraphs three and four of the previous page offer a positive way in which all our emotions may be handled. Here is a way of growth and integration which cannot but find its repercussions on those around us.

What do we mean by healing?

Several times we have spoken of the healing benefits of prayer. But what is it that we mean? Perhaps most people would answer that by healing is meant a restoration to bodily and mental health. This takes us part of the way, and often through prayer, and the consequent, deepening participation in the life-giving energies of the Holy Spirit (overcoming psychological blockages which may have been present) quite remarkable physical recovery takes place. But by healing we mean in the first place something deeper than restoration to physical health.

Consider these words from a Jungian analyst: 'The physician who settles for the removal of a diseased organ, or the psycho-therapist who settles for the extirpation of a complex is neglecting the health and welfare of his patient.'

That is a challenging thought. What lies behind it, of course, is that the diseased organ or complex is not in itself the evil but the symptom of what is really wrong.

We are led to reflect that real disease (dis-ease) lies behind all symptoms and is to be found in alienation or partial alienation from God. And so the road to our deepest healing lies in the deepening acceptance of God's forgiveness, a glad dependence upon God's grace, and openness of response in the way God is calling us. Prayer effects growth in these areas of our lives.

Our sickness may be used

It would be naive to suppose that physical health, here and now, is always to be seen as God's will.

God's concern is, as we have seen, for our deepest healing and it may well be that sickness, if normally only for a time, is a contributory factor, or even a necessary condition for our total healing.

In sickness we may be offered a temporary respite from the hectic activity of ordinary life, wherein may be found an opportunity for reflection, self-knowledge and penetration in depth by the Holy Spirit.

Or it may be that illness will draw out the compassionate side of our nature, leading us to be more patient and understanding of others.

Sickness may, too, be seen as a challenge to faith and courage through which the Holy Spirit may in an exceptional degree irradiate our lives.

It would be hard to see how one of the most courageous and inspiring people of our time, Dr Helen Keller, could have given more to humanity if her physical infirmities had been healed.

How about a neurosis?

Psychological illness, a neurosis for example, may also serve the cause of inner healing. We may believe that for some of the saints a neurotic condition contributed to their immense spiritual vitality.

Thus, Dom Oswald Sumner OSB observes: 'We can see that, in the spiritual life, it is quite possible to have, say, a neurosis at one level, yet at another we have a divine influence and a deepening of the whole spiritual life using perhaps the neurosis as one of its most powerful instruments.'

It is reasonable to suppose that St Paul's thorn in the flesh stemmed from a neurotic root. Some of us may draw courage from the thought.

It does not of course belittle St Paul, but, if anything, honours him the more, as being content for God's glory to accept his condition and see in it the secret of God's power.

'Most gladly, therefore, will I glory in my infirmities that the power of Christ may rest upon me.'[1]

A difficult tension to hold

None of this, however, should blind us to the fact that God's will for people is normally health in body and mind. It should simply warn us against the superficial view of healing which looks for it only in physical and mental fitness.

We must grasp that the most robust health is as nothing if its possessor is inwardly alienated from God, that such a person is in no sense healed in the Christian understanding of the word.

Nor should it be supposed that, ordinarily, growth in holiness and love of God and our fellow beings are not best assisted by soundness in mind and body.

We shall thus always be looking towards health, both for ourselves and others, at the same time learning to accept and turn to God's glory physical incapacity if complete health be denied.

This is not an easy tension to hold, but nothing less seems demanded of us.

There is mystery here

What a mystery lies at the heart of this subject! How often, for example, may we have noticed that people who are undoubtedly called by God to bring healing to others are themselves called to pass through pain and sickness.

Dorothy Kerin, brought back from the threshold of death, had later to experience much suffering in the preparatory years for her life work.

Godfrey Mowatt came to the healing ministry only after blindness had overtaken him, and later asked his friends not to pray for his cure as his ministry was strengthened by his infirmity.

Padre Pio endures the pain and physical incapacity placed on him by the stigmata, and thereby his ministry is transfigured.

Does it often appear that the babes in Christ, or those as yet unborn in him, are set free, while to the seasoned warriors comes the call to share more fully the fellowship and fruits of Christ's passion?

Certainly there is mystery here. We do well to be on our guard against facile suggestions that it is a want of faith or courage which keeps sick people from getting well. It may be that if we had more courage we would be in the same position ourselves. God may see that, given such an ordeal as theirs, we would simply crumple up and despair.

In the Eucharist there is true health

We are not to be discouraged, nor see it necessarily as a failure, if after prayer for healing no physical healing takes place.

Paul was not healed. Timothy's digestive problems presumably remained, the sickness of Epaphroditus seemingly hung in the balance for some while, and Paul had to leave his friend Trophimus sick at Miletum.[1]

We are to lay ourselves open to the power of the Holy Spirit as far as he enables us, and we must be content and humble enough to leave it at that.

In the Eucharist we are fed with the very life of the crucified, risen and glorified Christ, and in the possession of that life *is* health, whatever physical incapacities and infirmities may be ours.

We are to place no limit on God's power to bring us to health of body and mind, nor are we to doubt his love and wisdom (nor his power, though his power is no other than the power of love) if after seeking health we remain unwell.

Rather are we to seek to offer ourselves as we are, and to believe that God knows that our weakness, at least for the time being, provides the most favourable condition in which we can minister to one another, and in which real healing can go forward.[2]

Sleep is the gift of God

Earlier we quoted Brother Lawrence who said that those who have the 'gale of the Spirit' go forward even in sleep. Yet what a forgotten area of life is this! And most of us will spend more than twenty years asleep.

Sleep is not simply a way of passing from night-time until day. It makes a tremendous difference whether we approach it preparedly, or whether we take our negative and destructive emotions to bed with us.

The one who goes to bed with fear will wake with fear. The one who goes to bed with anger will wake with anger. And so we might go on. How wisely did Paul say: 'Do not let the sun go down upon your wrath!'

But, happily, the one who goes to bed in peace will wake in peace.

'He giveth his beloved sleep.' So runs the familiar verse. But it is better rendered: 'He giveth to his beloved in sleep.'

In sleep our physical, mental and spiritual energies are restored. And our psychic life is given harmony and balance through nature's mechanism of the dream.

'I will lay me down in peace and take my rest.' A period of unstrained relaxed prayer is the best preparation for a good night's sleep.

'Underneath are the everlasting arms.'

Relaxation a preparation for sleep

One of the best preparations for sleep is to lie flat on your back on the floor or some other hard surface.

Your legs should be slightly apart and your arms a little way from your body. Let the palms of your hands rest on the ground.

You may need a cushion. If so, pull it well in to your shoulders (not under them) so that the neck is supported and the head rests on it.

Take two or three good abdominal breaths to change the pattern of your breathing, and then breathe naturally.

Close your eyes lightly and speak to one arm gently and tell it to relax; then to the other arm; and to your hands and shoulders and face and jaw, and so on and on. The relaxation of one part of your body will assist the relaxation of all the rest.

If thoughts arise do not fight them but let them fall away, you meanwhile renewing your attention to your body. Continue for ten minutes or for as long as you need.

Use suitable prayers if you wish: 'Casting all your care upon him'; 'Into your hands I commend my spirit'; 'Underneath are the everlasting arms'.

Many now dependent on sleeping tablets will find their cure in this practice. But few will believe it until they have tried.

A new theology

True prayer springs from true theology. Perhaps we should have started our book here. The point is vital. If you are off target in your vision of God, your prayer life will suffer accordingly.

For most of my life I have believed that if I sinned against God and repented, God would forgive me.

This is good news. But the truth is yet better news. For God in fact forgives me before I repent, even though I can only appropriate his forgiveness after my repentance.

This is not just a new phraseology. It is a new theology. And because theology and life are inextricably woven, it is a new sociology as well.

For if we are to be children of our Father in heaven it follows that the manner of our loving must reflect his. Hence the spirit of forgiveness is to flow to all men and women everywhere.

Whether the other is able to receive it is another matter. But it does not belong to us to withdraw it.

Perhaps it is better to speak of reconciliation rather than forgiveness, as a reminder that we all stand in need of the forgiveness of one another.

The forgiveness of Jesus from the cross preceded any movement of sorrow or repentance on the part of those responsible for his death. It is in the knowledge of God's forgiving love always coming to meet us that our hearts are moved and our repentance is quickened.

A wrath-free God

We have spoken of a new theology. We must now ask what lies behind it.

It is the doctrine taught by Julian of Norwich that there is no wrath in God. 'God is the goodness that can know no anger, for he is nothing but goodness.'[1] Julian tells us this in one way or another no less than ten times, and says four times that it formed a part of each of her sixteen revelations.

Belief in a sometimes angry God, which is the truth of Christian tradition, should be seen as a relative truth only. Its strength is that it helps us to conserve certain important values concerning God, such as his abhorrence of evil and his passionate concern for our welfare. It also helps us to understand that in rejecting the love of God we are moving towards our own destruction.

For these reasons we must not lightly set it aside. Images are to be discarded only when we can move on to better ones. Otherwise we are liable to be left floundering in a spiritual vacuum.

Julian's truth is that the wrath is in us and not in God. She describes it as a perversity and opposition to peace and love. This wrath is quenched in the power of God's wrath-free love.

There is no wrath in God which consigns us to hell, but it is possible for our own wrath to do so.

Forgiving and forgetting

'I can forgive but I can never forget.' No doubt the worth of the saying depends on the tone of voice. But theologically speaking it is unexceptionable.

We do not have to forget. For Christians the greatest offence in the world's history was the crucifixion of its Lord. Far from forgetting the suffering and death of Jesus we enshrine it in the heart of the liturgy. And every time we say the Creed we recall his death.

But there is a type of forgetting which we are to exercise as Christians. We are right to forget the crucifixion of Jesus in the sense that we do not remember the offence *against* those who were responsible.

And this type of forgetting is what we mean by forgiveness.

It is a type of forgetting which softens the heart of the offender, leading to the repentance which allows forgiveness to be consummated.

'One should not expect to be forgiven because one has changed for the better; neither should one make such a change a condition for forgiving other people; it is only because one is forgiven, one is loved, that one can begin to change, not the other way round. And this we should never forget, though we always do.'[1]

'While God does not, and man dare not, demand repentance as a condition for *bestowing* pardon, repentance remains an essential condition for *receiving* it.'[2]

Allowing suffering to be creative

When you pray, let it be a settled habit of your mind that God's compassionate love rests upon you.

There is, we have affirmed, no wrath in God. The wrath is in us and not in God. It is the work of God's compassionate love to dissolve the wrath in ourselves.

It should not be thought, however, that to believe in a wrath-free God means that we do not suffer.

The perfecting of our penitence and the unveiling of our masks and pretences (even to ourselves) will involve suffering which may be deep and fearful.

God's compassion, then, does not mean that we do not suffer. What it means is this: that in our suffering God is on our side.

Our choice as Christians is not whether we suffer or whether we do not. Our choice is whether, given suffering, it shall be creative or destructive.

Suffering becomes creative when we unite ourselves in spirit with Christ's passion, thereby becoming sharers in his own redemptive work.

Suffering which is creative erodes our false self-love, chips away at our pride and works to establish the grace of humility.

Humility

Humility is the foundation of all virtues. No other virtue is possible without it. But there is not much we can do actively to acquire it.

It is a bit like relaxation. If you work at it too hard you become more tense. The art is in being able to allow it to happen.

So if you are too eager to take the lowest place, to submit without question, to do the lowly jobs, to hold back your opinion, it could be that the self in you which needs to die is in a subtle and secret manner being fed; and that under the mask of humility there may lie an unsuspected pride.

True humility is the by-product of adoration, praise and worship. It is something which steals in quietly while you are looking the other way.

True humility is an infused rather than an acquired virtue. It is worked in us through the patient endurance of events which make our self-love suffer.

Humility and self-knowledge go hand in hand. Thus St Teresa can say: 'Humility is truth.'

Benedicite

'God, of your goodness, give me yourself, for you are enough for me, and I can ask for nothing which is less which can pay you full worship. And if I ask anything which is less, always I am in want; but only in you do I have everything.'[1]

The words are from Julian of Norwich. It is easy to misunderstand them and to think that Julian is saying that so long as we have God, everything belonging to the natural order of creation can be left behind as though it had no relevance.

But Julian is not saying that. Julian is world affirming and not world denying. What she is saying is that in God all creation is given back to us, but now it is transformed because of our love relationship with him.

And so it is that she continues: 'God's goodness fills all his creatures and all his blessed works full, and endlessly overflows in them.'[2]

We do not love God more by loving his creation less. We are to love the things of God in God and for God. This is the fruit of contemplation. Everything is to be gathered up in God. This is to enter into the liberty which belongs to the children of God.

'As I see it,' (writes Julian), 'God is all that is good, has made all that is made, and loves all he has made. So he who loves all his fellow-Christians for God's sake, loves all that is made.'[3]

Appendix

Obtaining a rosary. Clearly, if you are to get full value from this book you will need a rosary. You may already have one, but if not, and you live in a sizeable town, there should be no problem. Rosaries can usually be bought at cathedral bookshops or at any branch of the SPCK. Most Roman Catholic bookshops sell them; and many other shops too.

You may expect to pay between £2 and £5, though some are priced well beyond that. There may be those of you for whom it is more convenient to buy from us at the Julian Shrine. We can usually offer to supply you promptly. We can send only one colour (which is black) and (currently) in the style illustrated in this book. The rosary is of medium size. If you order from us, please send a stamped addressed envelope with a cheque for £2.50 made payable to the Julian Shrine. Your envelope should be at least 5 in x 4 in (13 cm × 10 cm) and stamped for the first postage stage. Post to the Chaplain at the Julian Shrine, c/o All Hallows, Rouen Road, Norwich NR1 1QT.

If you would like your rosary blessed at the Julian Shrine, please say so and we shall be glad to do this for you.

Groups for silent contemplative prayer. There are many groups which meet for silent corporate prayer under the auspices of the 'Julian Meetings'. At the time of writing there are about 150 such groups, so there should be a good chance of one being near you.

The 'Julian Meetings' also issue three times a year a paper with articles on the spiritual life and information on the work of the groups. The movement is firmly Christ-centred, but has no denominational boundaries or formal membership requirements. For particulars write to Mrs Hilary Burn, 'Julian Meetings', 5 Geale's Crescent, Alton, Hants GU34 2ND (telephone 0420–83088).

Notes

In the notes below, abbreviations are used as follows:

CW for *Revelations of Divine Love*, trans. Clifton Wolters (Penguin Classics 1973)
EC and JW for *Julian of Norwich. Showings*, trans. Edmund Colledge OSA and James Walsh SJ (SPCK 1979)
EIL and *IEL* for *Enfolded in Love* and *In Love Enclosed*. Both books are published by Darton, Longman and Todd and consist of daily readings from Julian of Norwich, ed. Robert Llewelyn, trans. Sheila Upjohn
RDL for *Revelations of Divine Love* by Julian of Norwich

Page	Note	
xi	1	I owe the phrase to Bishop John Taylor
xii	1	Quoted from Evelyn Underhill, *Worship* (Nisbet 1936)
2	1	Origen
11	1	*EIL*, p. 2 (*RDL*, ch. 4)
	2	EC and JW, ch. 25
12	1	*IEL*, p. 24 (*RDL*, ch. 18)
	2	Noel Dermot O'Donoghue SJ, *Heaven in Ordinarie* (T. and T. Clark 1979)
13	1	*EIL*, p. 2 (*RDL*, ch. 4)
	2	*EIL*, p. 8 (*RDL*, ch. 7)
	3	EC and JW, ch. 13 (the Shorter Text)
18	1	Shirley Hughson OHC, *Contemplative Prayer* (Holy Cross Press 1955)
25	1	St Paul (Rm 8:22)
	2	Bishop Gore
	3	See Ian Wilson, *The Turin Shroud* (Gollancz 1978). A brief reference is also made in Ian Wilson's article 'The evidence for Jesus' in *In Search of Christianity*, ed. Tony Moss (Firethorn Press 1986)
30	1	Maisie Ward's book *The Splendour of the Rosary* (Sheed and Ward 1946), now out of print, brings together Fra Angelico's paintings covering the fifteen mysteries. The reproductions are in black and white

Notes

31	1	Quoted, with some adaptation, from the above book
45	1	1 Tm 4:4
	2	William Blake
47	1	St Augustine on Psalm 37
50	1	CW, ch. 41
51	1	Author not traced
	2	*EIL*, p. 5 (*RDL*, ch. 6)
	3	St Augustine
52	1	Mt 7:7
53	1	Verrier Elwyn, *Richard Rolle*
	2	St Ignatius Loyola, *Spiritual Exercises*, 1st week, section iv (London 1919)
56	1	Elaine Pagels, *The Gnostic Gospels* (Weidenfeld and Nicolson 1979)
61	1	Plotinus
64	1	William Barnes (1801–86), *Mater Dolorosa*
70	1	2 Co 12:9
73	1	2 Co 12:9; 1 Tm 5:23; Ph 2:25–30; 2 Tm 4:20
	2	In this reading, and the previous five, I have quoted or adapted from Robert Llewelyn, *Prayer and Healing* (Julian Shrine Publication 1978)
77	1	*IEL*, p. 51 (*RDL*, ch. 46)
78	1	Metropolitan Anthony of Sourozh MD, DD, *Meditations on a Theme* (Mowbray 1971)
	2	Dorothy Sayers, *Unpopular Opinions* (London 1951)
81	1	EC and JW, ch. 5
	2	Ibid.
	3	*EIL*, p. 9 (*RDL*, ch. 9)